D0590740

# Cautionary Tales for Grown-Ups

# CauTIONaRY

## TaLeS for GROWN -UPs

### BY CHRIS ADDISON

ILLUSTRATED BY ADAM HOWLING

HODDER &
STOUGHTON

First published in Great Britain in 2006 by Hodder & Stoughton
A division of Hodder Headline

The right of Chris Addison to be identified as the Author of the Work has been asserted by him
in accordance with the Copyright, Designs and Patents Act 1988.

A Hodder & Stoughton Book

2

A CIP catalogue record for this title is available from the British Library

ISBN 0 340 92070 X
978 0 340 92070 I

Typeset in Centaur MT

Printed and bound in Great Britain by Mackays of Chatham Ltd, Chatham Kent

Hodder Headline's policy is to use papers that are natural, renewable and recyclable products and
made from wood grown in sustainable forests. The logging and manufacturing processes are
expected to conform to the environmental regulations of the country of origin.

Hodder & Stoughton Ltd
A division of Hodder Headline
338 Euston Road
London NWI 3BH

For Jo, who already knows these things,
And for Jacob, who'll learn them soon enough.

# STOP THERE, DEAR SHOPPER.

In your hand,
Fresh plucked from shelf or twirling stand,
You hold a volume which intends
Society should make amends
For all the little nameless crimes
Which damnify these Modern Times.
Within these covers you will read
Of negligence and evil deed,
Of miscreants both big and small
And what sad fates befell them all:
A man who simply would not vote,
A woman killed by whaling boat,
A man who talked in business-speak,
A woman on a diet a week
And many other boobs besides.
A word of warning, though – these guides
To living well are missing one;
I have, when all is said and done,
Forborne for taste's sake to relate
The single foulest tale: the fate
Which once befell, as well it ought,
The man who browsed but never bought.

# Cautionary Tales for Grown-ups

# RAY, WHO REFUSED TO VOTE AND LOST EVERYTHING

There upon his sagging couch,
  Lazy Raymond – sloven, slouch
    And dullard – whiles away his time
      And checks his fingernails for grime,
        Or picks his nose and – lacking charm –
          Wipes snot all down the sofa's arm.
          He'll stir his stumps to eat or piss;
          Beyond such things, his motto's this:
          'As sure as my name's Lazy Ray,
          This couch is where I'm going to stay.'

Now, polling morning came to dawn.
The beer cans out on Ray's front lawn
Were glinting in the morning shine,
As up the path at half past nine
A canvasser – one Seymour Trout –
Approached, to Get The Voter Out.
Reluctant Ray came to his door;
Said he: 'The whole thing's such a bore.
Since none of you lot speak to me,
My party shall be Apathy.'

Thus disappointed, Trout withdrew.
Ray shut the door and went to stew
Upon his couch.  He squeezed a spot
And flicked the pus into a pot.
He never went that day to vote.
(The chances always were remote.)
Nor did he see this come to pass:
A man he thought an utter ass
Was voted in to Number Ten
Before Ray went to bed again.

For he, alas, was not alone;
  Ten million apathetic clones
    Chose also to ignore the Poll.
     The voter shortfall took its toll.
      Next day – too late – they realised
       That now a man whom they despised
        Had won, whilst they, slumped in their chairs,
         Had idly groomed their nasal hairs.
          Yet none of them would take the blame
           Or feel the smallest twinge of shame.

           The weeks drew on, moons waxed and waned,
          And with the mandate he'd obtained
         The gentleman in Downing Street,
        Who'd found his governmental feet,
       Decided to enact a bill
      The Opposition couldn't kill:
     Messy gardens, snotty couches,
    Dullards, slovens, slatterns, slouches –
   All of them would now be taxed.
  More weeks drew on, moons waned and waxed.

The bill was law, fait accompli,
Ray and his clones had failed to see
They'd score this terrible own goal
The day they chose to snub the Poll.
Though Raymond and the rest were skint,
The Government had hearts of flint
And bailiffs came, in lieu of pay,
To cart poor Raymond's couch away.
He sighed and said, 'Still, there's no law
To stop me sitting on the floor.'

But Raymond's floor was cold and hard
And Raymond's arse was largely lard
And after sitting in this style
A time, the lad developed piles.
So now he stands all day instead
(The bailiffs also took his bed)
And spends his time – with still less charm –
In wiping snot down his own arm,
And with sore feet accepts this fact:
It's all his fault – he failed to act.

And so, dear child, as Seymour Trout
Would doubtless say, were he about,
Whatever be your party's hue –
Green, Purple, Yellow, Red or Blue –
At each election get your coat
And put it on and go and vote.

# THE RESIDENTS OF
## TAUNTON STREET, WHO COVERED
### THEIR HOUSES WITH CHRISTMAS DECORATIONS

Rowetta, Deirdre, Kevin, Eric, Jimbo, Debs and Pete
Lived happily as neighbours on the same suburban street.
Their civil co-existence and their usual good cheer
Were set aside with venom, though, for six weeks every year.
On the sixteenth of November, each, quite giddy with delight,
Would wrap their house in rope lights and illuminate the night
With six-foot Santas, snowmen, deer — the standard 'Xmas' crew —
And sundry other flashing tat they'd bought at B&Q.

Unspoken competition will get quickly out of hand,
Which moral can be proven by the fate of this dull band,
For annual improvements to each household's own array
(viz. brighter, bigger, gaudier and costlier displays)
Meant pretty soon that after dark their road became so bright
It looked like (from the air, at least) two long, straight strips of light.
Rowetta, Deirdre, Kevin, Eric, Jimbo, Debs and Pete
All died when Flight 4192 touched down on Taunton Street.

# THE GLOUCESTERSHIRE HORSE CLUB, WHO POSED NAKED FOR A CHARITY CALENDAR

The curse of our times, if you asked me to name one,
I'd tell you – please don't think me rude –
Is the modish desire of the folk of this nation
To pose for a snap in the nude.

A charity wheeze of quite splendid intentions
Which now has got so out of hand
That every third granny has stripped in her kitchen
And hidden her wrinkles with cans.

But if you're convinced such a novelty calendar's
Really the thing for your cause,
Pay heed to the fate of the Gloucestershire Horse Club
Whose story may well give you pause:

Miss January started things off with a flyer
Whilst sitting astride bales of hay,
For some of the stalks were a little bit loose and she's
Picking them out to this day.

The next month, Anne Wilkes posed as Lady Godiva
Buck naked atop her own horse,
Who, shocked at the sight, simply whinnied and bolted
And threw her off into the gorse.

For March, by request, Keith the stable lad modelled,
All wreathed in the coils of a hose.
He tripped on a loop whilst assembling his features,
Fell forward and fractured his nose.

April, as months go, of course is the cruellest,
Especially if you're poor Meg;
She angered a swan on a shoot by the river
Who countered by breaking her leg.

Before she arrived for her own photo session,
Miss May had no more than a cough –
She left with a chestful of bronchopneumonia
From splashing about in a trough.

And matters did not take a turn for the better
When dear Miss June came to do hers;
A chain of events meant she severed a nipple
Whilst posing behind secateurs.

July wasn't great to the yard owner, Gordon,
Who lounged on an old drystone wall,
The coping of which was a little haphazard –
He can't move one foot now at all.

And August, September, October, November
Continued in much the same vein:
Two girls went to hospital, one went to Borstal,
The fourth lost the use of her brain.

So surely their luck must have changed for December?
You'd think so, but don't hold your breath –
A Christmas tableau with a whole herd of horses
Resulted in seventeen deaths.

The Gloucestershire Horse Club is scouting for members
To make up the shortfall on subs.
The moral is this: Things like charity nude shoots
Are ideas best left in the pub.

# ROWLEY, WHO CROSSED ROADS
## DELIBERATELY SLOWLY

Man, twenty-eight, haughty cool, name of Rowley,
Crossed the road always annoyingly slowly.
He waited till cars were incredibly near
Then sauntered across with an arrogant sneer,
And by this expedient – this was the plan –
He aimed to display to us he was The Man.
His end, though, was tragic; he dashed out his brains –
It turns out you can't do the same thing with trains.

# MATTHEW, WHO ONLY TEXTED

See this chap?  He's Matthew Dawling.
Matthew Dawling loves to text.
This he does instead of calling,
Leaving friends and family vexed.
Call it lazy, call it shrewd,
They all call it bloody rude.

Matt won't even pick his phone up
If it ever starts to ring.
Not, I'll grant you, very grown up,
Really not at all the thing.
He just waits until you've gone,
Texts you back and carries on.

Through this lack of conversation
Matthew's voice begins to change,
Suffering a decimation
Of his former vocal range.
Strange to say, he – like a text –
Has no vowels. Whatever next?

Though his voice has fallen victim
To a consonantal drift,
Matthew won't let that affect him –
Overall, he's not too miffed.
As it is he doesn't speak
More than once or twice a week.

Sometimes, though, you find the need to
Be quite clearly understood,
Otherwise no one pays heed to
What you say, and that's no good.
Matthew learns this far too late
At the hands of cruel fate:

Set upon by local yobbos,
Matthew tries to cry for 'Hlp!'
Not a chance – nobody near knows
What it means, this vowelless yelp.
Thus he draws his final breath,
Thn thy kck pr Mtt 2 dth.

# ADVICE TO A YOUNG MAN

## ON GOING INTO THE WORLD

At last you're an adult, at last you are leaving
To find a career and a home and a wife,
But, child, heed my words, for this world is deceiving;
It's hard for a fellow to live a good life.
So now as you stand on the edge of adventure,
Anxious to soar to the sky from the nest,
Allow me, my son, if you would, just to venture
These words of advice, which I can't overstress:
Don't murder old ladies – you wouldn't have liked it
If someone had done the same thing to your gran.
Don't ply girls with booze when you've previously spiked it
Then bundle them off in the back of a van.
Don't buy packs of Semtex from shady old villains
Then detonate charges at public events.
Don't package your mucus as cheap penicillin
Then sell it at fairgrounds to gullible gents.
And nobbling children to sell into slavery
Simply because you are short of a bob,
Quite rightly, I feel, is regarded as knavery;
If you need money, apply for a job.

The practice of genocide has its supporters –
  Dictators and despots and one or two kings –
    Observe, though, the view which prevails in most quarters:
      To put it succinctly, it's not the done thing.
        Don't heckle the Pope when he's hearing confession,
          Don't loiter in houses of risqué repute,
            Don't burgle, don't swindle, don't practise aggression,
              Don't flatter, don't libel, don't pillage, don't loot.
                Above all of these here's my final dictation:
                  Don't formulate fatuous, half-thought-through views
                    Then take up the BBC's dumb invitation
                      To email them in to the Six O'Clock News.

# AMELIA, WHO THREW A
# CIGARETTE BUTT FROM A CAR

A charming day in Ballygill.
  The sun was shining on the hill
  And birds were skirling in the sky
  As all at once there happened by
  Amelia in a blue Corvette,
  Dragging on a cigarette.

She sucked the baccy to the butt
And, brushing ash from off her gut,
She nonchalantly yawned and wound
The Corvette's offside window down
And, with the manners of a chimp,
Lightly threw away the dimp.

The fag-end cartwheeled, sparked and lay
Upon the tarmacked carriageway
Until a classic Irish gust
Blew it with the leaves and dust
Along the gutter, whence some rain
Nicely sluiced it down a drain.

The butt was swallowed by a rat,
Mangy, manky, rank and fat,
Whose views on what he'd count as food
Were hugely broad and deeply crude;
For him this litter off the street
Made a rare, if chewy, treat.

But once it passed the creature's jaw,
The flotsam settled in his craw
And bunged him up till, blind with pain,
He scuttled off along the drain
And, never knowing where he went,
Scrambled up a nearby vent

Which opened on Amelia's yard
And there he fell upon a shard
Of bottle-glass as she passed by,
And, giving out a rodent cry,
The fetid fellow, cruelly cursed,
Breathed his very last and burst.

Brains and gizzards, guts and hair
Showered foully through the air;
Last to fall, the soggy dimp,
Swollen, slick with blood and limp,
Arced its little way through space
And landed on Amelia's face.

In her haste to reach a tap
And clean herself of ratty crap,
She slipped and fell against a pile
Of terracotta roofing tiles,
On which there stood an open tin
She used for storing paraffin.

It fell, sparked, caught, then singed her head
But — worse — it lit the nearby shed,
 Which soon was quite engulfed in flames
 (A glut of creosote was blamed).
 Amelia, dazed, lay on the ground
 And barely heard the crackling sound.

 The conflagration spread in time
 All along the washing line
 And reached the house.  The back-door porch
 Ignited like a tinder torch —
 The kitchen first and then the hall,
 The bedrooms, bathrooms, lounge and all

 Were set ablaze.  Amelia woke
 To see her whole house wreathed in smoke,
 So with her mobile summoned aid
 By calling out the fire brigade,
 Who came and did their job quite well
But only left a brittle shell.

And as Amelia now beheld
 The ruin where she once had dwelled,
 A mid-migration guillemot
 Alighted on the chimney-pot,
 Which, loosened by both fire and gull,
 Fell and crushed Amelia's skull.

A charming day in Ballygill.
 The sun still shining on the hill,
 The birds still skirling in the sky,
 As all at once a hearse came by
 To haul Amelia out of sight.
 You know what? Serve her bloody right.

# GERALD QUIMBY,

## WHO PROTESTED AT EVERYTHING

Have you heard of Gerald Quimby?
Quite the most appalling NIMBY,
PhD in demonstrating,
Cavilling and remonstrating.
In re: any proposition
Gerald was in opposition;
Staring at you long and hard
He'd bellow, 'Not in *my* backyard!'

Gerry's shed was full of banners,
Placards, paints and twelve-month planners
(Blank, so when the breakfast news
Reported things which in his view
Could not be borne, a morning's work
Amidst the grow-bags and the murk
And he, by lunch, could from thin air
Stage demos in the village square).

Quimby and his troupe of grumps –
Sour-faced majors, Barboured frumps,
Tweed-bound Luddites, manger dogs,
Churls and would-be demagogues,
Those for whom there's barely use
And positively no excuse –
Stamped and spat with little grace
And regularly won their case.

Build a prison?  Not round here;
Gerald had instilled the fear
In every local round about
Of convicts nightly getting out.
Immigrant reception centre?
Not a chance; the Chief Dissenter –
One G. Quimby – snuffed that threat
And barely even broke a sweat.

'Clearly, these things must be built,'
Owned Gerry, yet he felt no guilt
In letting others take the brunt,
The sanctimonious little runt.
Whatever the proposed erection,
Quimby found an apt objection.
Not one blemish, not one blot
Would uglify his little plot.

Build a school? 'My dear, the noise
Of all those hoodied little boys!'
Swimming pool? 'The stench of chlorine
Aggravates poor Auntie Maureen.'
A convent then — you can't object.
'Ha! Au contraire, you're incorrect;
Nuns attract a goddish crowd
Whose psalmic drone is far too loud.'

Not content with getting canned
Whatever other folk had planned,
Quimby eyed existing work
And set his knee to Full Speed Jerk;
The church, for starters, had to go
(Its spire might buckle under snow),
Then butcher, baker, betting shop
And bank all got the Quimby chop.

Before too long, where once had been
A village round a charming green,
Stood nothing but a silly man,
Stacking placards in a van;
No shops, no phones, no food, no roads,
No nothing but his own abode.
Cut off, alone and ill-supplied,
To no one's great surprise, he died.

Thus the fate of Gerald Quimby;
Here's the moral: Be a NIMBY
If you like, but all you'll save
Your backyard for will be your grave.

# GASPARD HAMMER,

## WHO DRESSED TOO YOUNG

Mark the tale of Gaspard Hammer (Eton, Cantab. (BA, Hons.)),
Once a television bigwig of renown,
Feted darling of the BBC and fellow of St John's –
Former modish beau and young blade about town.
He had vanity aplenty
And this simple failing meant he
Dressed, though pushing fifty-one,
Like someone nearer twenty.

Though he'd grey hair at his temples, though he'd lines upon his face,
Though he had to get up every night to pee,
Shirts and sober ties and jackets in his wardrobe found no place
(Nor did pants, for he preferred to wander free).
He would say: 'I hate convention
And declare it my intention
To continue wearing what I please
Until I draw my pension.'

So he chaired important meetings wearing baggy, boarders' shorts,
He turned up to work with dyed and spiky hair,
He wore jeans whose cloth had been designed for use by astronauts
To the theatre, or when dining with the mayor.
With his friends this affectation
Met distinct disapprobation
(Though they kept that to themselves
To avoid his indignation).

On wandering through Shepherd's Bush to go and buy the *Face*,
Gaily swigging diet cola from a can,
Gaspard came upon the woman who would cause his fall from grace
As she scouted round for truants in a van.
Being cursed with failing vision,
She had come to a decision
To determine age through clothing,
Which she did with imprecision.

On espying Gaspard strolling down the street without a care,
She assumed at once he must be on the lam.
In his black nu-metal T-shirt and his baggy denim flares
He appeared though he were fresh sprung from the pram.
So despite his protestations
And his vulgar imprecations
He was bundled in the wagon
And then taken down the station.

Now, the sergeant, it would seem, was either lazy or quite bored,
And – as Gaspard found – he wasn't on the take.
He was unimpressed by Hammer's claims of knowing several lords
And repeated cries of, 'This is some mistake!'
Thus, now locked up in a cell
And entreated to sleep well,
Gaspard didn't, so by six a.m.
He really looked like hell.

In the morning, poor old Gaspard found himself before the bench,
Dressed in stale – albeit highly trendy – clothes,
He was bleary-eyed, unshaven and possessed of quite a stench
(Indicated by the JP's wrinkled nose).
Said the beak, 'Now, I opine
This absenting little swine
Is deserving of a punishment
Much greater than a fine.'

'But I'm fifty!' blurted Gaspard, 'I've been decades out of school,'
And he offered up an ID card as proof.
Still the magistrate's demeanour remained unimpressed and cool
(One reporter claimed it bordered on aloof):
'I'd say that by the sound of it
That's certainly a counterfeit
And so, like all your other lies,
This court takes no account of it.'

When the judgment came, poor Gaspard found it worse than he had feared
And he whimpered as they took him from the dock.
Now, as Borstal's only inmate who can grow himself a beard,
All he does all day is mutter and break rocks.
What this little story shows
Is this moral, I suppose:
You should always act the age you are
When putting on your clothes.

# MIRANDA,
## WHO GOT A TATTOO

Just after turning twenty-two,
Miranda got a small tattoo.
She did so to achieve these ends:
She wanted to be like her friends
And demonstrate to you and me
Her individuality.

Miranda had a man in Rye
Ink a dolphin on her thigh
And plunge a needle through her skin –
She bore this torture with a grin.
The finished thing she said was 'sweet'
And asked the man for a receipt.

The years went by, Miranda's fab
Mid-twenties figure turned to flab –
And so it should; to grave from crêche
That is the usual way of flesh –
So now (this made her feel quite sick)
The dolphin looked like Moby Dick.

On holiday in Norway's fjords
Miranda, heedless, swam towards
A whaling boat which went about.
The look-out shouted, well, 'Look out!'
For he, of course, had chanced to spy
The monster on Miranda's thigh.

Sad to say at just past noon
Miranda met the boat's harpoon.
It's such a shame, though I'll admit
They didn't waste a single bit:
For even now they use, the scamps,
Miranda's oil for lighting lamps.

# THE MIMSY-GORES, WHO RODE ABOUT TOWN IN A 4X4

Consider, please, Pippa and Sam Mimsy-Gore,
She: high-flying banker, he: doctor at law,
Suburbia's finest. Their brood having hatched,
They've moved to a light, spacious, semi-detached

And filled it with treasures most prized by their ilk:
Rough carpets of rattan, soft cushions of silk,
A study, a romper room, worktops of chrome
And such as befits the best middle-class home.

And out on the driveway at *Chez* Mimsy-Gore
There stands – monolithic – a tan four-by-four
Of which they have lately become the proud owners
By using Pip's frankly obscene Christmas bonus.

And, oh, how they love it, this behemoth car.
'It's not that we use it to drive all that far,
Just Waitrose and crèche runs and things of that sort,'
Drones Sam. 'Really most of our trips are quite short.'

Alas, that's quite true, for this beast of a jeep —
A fortune to buy, and to run hardly cheap —
This gas-guzzling, four-wheeled, tyrannosaur rig,
This air-fouling redefinition of 'big',

This all-terrain monster, more meant for the mud,
For battling through bog-land and plashing through flood,
That cuts through rough earth like a teaspoon through chutney
Has barely set tyre more than two miles from Putney.

Its trips around town meet contemptuous snorts,
Quite often it features in travel reports
For blocking the traffic on every side.
(Still, no surprise there – it's about three lanes wide.)

Through all of this Pippa and Sam seem quite heedless –
Prevailing opinion may damn it as needless
Extravagance, owning this country-style car,
The act of an insecure, urban bourgeois,

Such views, though, just leave them a little nonplussed:
'With family cars, it's an absolute must
To make sure they're roomy, to make sure they're tough,
With bull-bars and suchlike,' claims Pippa. 'Enough

To satisfy fully the jumpiest Dad
Viz. comfort and safety for his little lad.
Of course I'd be *frantic* if (heaven forfend!)
A knock from our car brought another child's end,

But say what you like – you can wail, you can moan –
One's major concern is the good of one's own,
And if that's thought selfish, well there it is – sorry.'
And off huffs Pip, driving her family lorry.

Thus Pippa and Sam square their conscience with ease;
Their fortune is all, others' sorrow hard cheese –
That foul status symbol with bull-bars up front
Is all for the good of their own little runt.

And what of the beetroot-faced bundle of joy
That warrants such treatment – the Mimsy-Gore boy?
Yes, what of him? Is he a sweet little lad?
A paragon? Calm? Always good, never bad?

Alas, no, not so, for this three-year-old bloater,
Replete in striped jacket and nursery boater,
Has spent his short years in pursuit of one dream:
The world's loudest, longest and highest-pitched scream.

He's brattish, he's spoilt, he's uncommonly fat.
His parents, of course, can't see any of that –
Pip mothers him, smothers him, fills him with sweets,
Sam showers his first-born with trinkets and treats.

Thus each day his tantrums grow steadily worse,
His yelling gets louder, his sulks more perverse.
'It's not that Nathaniel is selfish or vile,'
They'll tell you. 'It's just he's a *sensitive* child.'

Now one day, this pair and their blazer-clad banshee,
Encouraged by Pip, on advice from a man she
Was friends with at work, took a trip across town.
Their mission was simple: they went to track down

A chap whom Pip's colleague had praised to the skies
For selling off cheaply his ample supplies
Of Philippe Starck taps, Le Corbusier chairs
And bijou, steel candlesticks (singles and pairs).

Designer goods sold at such laughable prices
Perhaps is the first among middle-class vices.
That's why Pip and Sam were quite happy to stray
From Putney – this once – to Mile End, far away.

The Saturday traffic was worse than they'd thought.
The GPS system which Sam had just bought
Could offer no succour: 'There's just no free route.
At this rate we'll all have to sleep in the boot,'

Whined Pippa. Snapped Sam: 'Don't exaggerate, dear.
I'll find a way through this, you'll see. Never fear!'
He spun the wheel clockwise – the car inched towards
A side-street, half clogged up with scaffolding boards.

The alley was narrow, the four-by-four wide,
With barely an inch-worth of clearance each side.
'How's *that* for smart driving?' said Sam. Pippa winced.
It seemed she for one remained far from convinced.

Quite right she was, too, for what lay round the bend,
Though neither one guessed, was their ultimate end.
Priest, write your eulogy; clean your suit, mourner –
Our story will end when Sam turns the next corner.

'The general direction we want is north-east,'
Said Sam as he manfully wrestled the beast
To the left, down a road slimmer still than the last,
Through which there was no way this car could have passed.

It proved to be so; a few feet further in
Came a crunch and a scrape and a terrible din,
The narrowing walls met the sides of the truck
And the Mimsy-Gore tribe found themsleves wholly stuck.

'Try forwards! Try backwards! Try flooring the gas!'
Nagged Pip. 'Really, Sam, you incompetent ass.'
Sam, reddening now, grew increasingly flustered,
'Oh, do shut up, woman!' he pompously blustered.

But what could he do? Because, try as he might,
Sam just couldn't move them – the car was stuck tight.
He shouted at Pippa, she yelled back at him,
Using words like 'divorce' and 'amoeba' and 'dim'.

So picture them there – they're quite stuck where they are,
And the doors are pinned shut – they can't exit the car.
Worse still, though, their son's in the back of the jeep.
Two minutes ago he was soundly asleep.

The shriek of torn metal, Mum howling at Dad,
Have served to arouse the irascible lad.
Incensed at this unscheduled end to his dreams,
The bloater lets fly with his highest-pitched scream.

It starts as a barely-perceptible hum,
As little Nat warms up his three-year-old lungs.
It rises in seconds through gurgle and yell
To the sound of the damned in the circles of hell

And doesn't stop there. The car starts to vibrate.
Pip tries now to calm him. Too bad, she's too late.
The howling gets louder – it soon comes to pass
That the force of the hissy fit shatters the glass.

The windows explode, but Nat's not stopping there –
Without even pausing to take in more air
He cranks up the volume again and a dull
Sensation begins at the base of Sam's skull.

Pip feels it as well and the pain starts to spread
Till a migraine-like throbbing encases their heads.
They plead with their son for an end to the din,
But this is his moment – Nat's not giving in.

His eyes are alight – it's his favourite game
And he knows he's within just an ace of his aim.
Just one final push will achieve his great dream:
The world's finest outburst – the scream de la scream.

The pounding gets worse in the Mimsy-Gore brains,
They've never before felt such terrible pain.
Their hands clasp their heads and their eyes are shut tight;
They pray for an end and an end is in sight.

The volume and pitch reach a critical mass,
Their skulls start to splinter and crack like the glass,
And there in a jeep in an East London road,
Three Mimsy-Gore skulls give a pop, then explode.

So here ends the story of Pippa and Sam,
Their truculent son and their ludicrous van.
If it's morals you're after, my favourite by far
Is: Exercise caution when buying a car.

# TO A GAP YEAR STUDENT,
## RETURNING FROM HIS TRAVELS

Why yes, I can tell you've been over the sea,
Now wiser at nineteen than I'll ever be,
But if you get punched holding forth over lunch,
Just don't you come running to me.

# MELANIE, WHO SPEED DATED

Miss Melanie Grime, a committed speed dater,
Would barely say 'Hi,' before 'Right, see you later.'
She courted a series of desperate hunks
In hopelessly whistle-stop five-minute chunks.
Now, one day Miss Melanie, much to her shock,
Fell hard for a soft-spoken lawyer named Jock.
No sooner, though, had these young lovebirds got hitched
Than Melanie felt the old Five-Minute Itch.
It can't have been more than half an hour later
She'd split up with Jock and eloped with a waiter.
And, much as she loved him then, come time for tea
Her number of husbands had risen to three.
The following evening the total was ten,
Then fourteen, then twenty, then thirty-six, then . . .

Well, then came a bailiff who formally served
Miss Grime with some papers she fully deserved:
Her exes, it seemed, had established a faction,
The purpose of which was a civil class action.
The judge who presided, as low as this sounds,
Awarded them only five million pounds,
But Melanie worked all the hours that God sends
To pay off the debt and to make them amends.
And since she was working, she hadn't the time
(A matter of horror to Melanie Grime)
For any speed dating or meeting new men;
She worked, went home, slept, got up, went back again.
At last, desiccated, defeated, dismayed,
Miss Melanie Grime left this world an old maid.

MORAL:

If ever you speed date, like Melanie Grime,
It's best if you marry them one at a time.

# JIM, WHO FLY-TIPPED

You've heard me talk of Lazy Ray
Who stayed home on election day?
Well, meet his brother, Lazy Jim –
Old Ray's a treat compared to him.
For decades now Jim's wife had moaned
That everything the couple owned
Was tatty, worn or past its prime.
She begged him, 'Jim, it *must* be time,
We've been here years – it's not too late
To gut this place and renovate.'

In time her carping grew so shrill
It made Jim feel a little ill,
So, heavy both of gut and heart,
He thought he'd make a gentle start
And, sitting in the musty gloom,
He ordered for the living room
A brand new set of everything –
New couch, new chairs, new shelves. The thing
He hadn't thought about was where
He'd put the ones already there.

He didn't want a costly skip
And as for driving to the tip
Himself, he thought he'd rather go
And barbecue his little toe.
At last an answer came to mind
Quite typical of Jimmy's kind
And one which he found hard to beat:
He'd put them outside in the street;
The council would, as is their way,
Send men to take the stuff away.

So first the sofa, then the lamp,
Then the carpet (slightly damp),
The clock, the TV stand, a load
Of chairs were dumped out in the road.
A stool came next and then a range
Of rugs which had developed mange,
And shelves – devoid of any books –
He'd used as makeshift inglenooks.
With faux-chrome legs, glass-topped and vast,
The coffee table came out last.

It seemed to Jim the job was done
But from his window later on
He saw the chairs were occupied.
The lamp was on and set beside
The sofa, which some stranger's hand
Had pointed at the TV stand.
And as he watched, he understood
That what he saw could bode no good –
It was, he thought with rueful frown,
A gypsy family bedding down.

He called the council right away.
A man without the least delay
Was sent with a theodolite
(A special one, which works at night),
A questionnaire, some legal texts,
A Bible and a roll of flex
To map the land and how it lay.
Said he: 'Well, Bye-law 14 (a)
Stroke (p), pertaining to such sites,
Awards these gypsies squatters' rights.'

'This judgment, I'm afraid, implies,
When viewed through purely legal eyes,
That though it was not your intention
To build your house a front extension,
That stuff out on the pavement counts
And so I must demand amounts
Of council tax – the highest band,
As per the statutes of the land –
For what now in the strictest sense
Constitutes a residence.'

'And furthermore,' the man went on
(And on and – if I'm honest – on),
'Since no building plans were lodged
And all permissions have been dodged,
I must impose a penalty
Of – wait a moment, let me see –
Ten thousand pounds. Does that sound right?
Of course it does. Oh, well. Goodnight.'
With that, he vanished through the door
And Jimmy fainted to the floor.

Lazy Jim could not afford a
Single thing he had on order
Once the fine and tax were paid,
And so, I'm very much afraid,
He, like his brother Ray before,
Was doomed to sit upon the floor
And contemplate for endless days
The stupid error of his ways –
A fitting outcome for a chump
Who used the highway as a dump.

NOTE:
For Mrs Lazy Jim, his wife,
Dear reader, do not be dismayed;
She found herself a better life
And ran off with a gypsy maid.

# JUSTIN, AN ARROGANT CYCLIST

Justin is a cyclist,
Justin goes by bike,
Justin thinks he has the right to ride it where he likes.

Justin's eco-friendly,
Justin's very green,
Justin thinks that's like a dispensation from the Queen.

Justin rides on pavements,
Justin jumps the lights,
Justin doesn't give a fig for anyone in sight.

Justin thinks they're lazy,
Justin thinks they're dim,
Justin thinks the only one who does his bit is him.

Justin's quite phlegmatic,
Justin's quite blasé,
Justin doesn't recognise he has no right of way.

Justin shouts at lorries,
Justin curses cars,
Justin swears at children on the crossing by the Spar.


Justin swerves past mothers,
Justin startles grans,
Justin goes where every form of transport has been banned.


Justin thinks he's splendid,
Justin thinks he's it,
Justin doesn't get that he makes other people spit.


Justin understands now,
Justin's grasp's improved,
Justin's gone to A&E to get a pump removed.

# FIONA AND DAVE,

## WHO HAD A WACKY WEDDING

Once both agreed that they should wed,
Fiona turned to Dave and said:
'Ours has been a *crazy* ride,
So when our bond is unified
We shouldn't have the usual guff –
A registrar or church – that stuff
Is far too normal.' Dave agreed:
'It seems to me that what we need
Is something different – nothing tacky –
Something out-to-lunch and wacky.
Our wedding must show everyone
That Dave and Fi are Lots Of Fun.'
Bristling with anticipation,
Dave and Fi sent invitations:
'Join us at the aerodrome!!
(Party later on at home!!!!)'

Their wedding day was, oh dear me,
The last that they would ever see,
For as their guests all stood around
Secure and safe on solid ground,
The happy couple, silly coots,
Decked out in nuptial parachutes,
Embarked the kind of aeroplane
That doesn't bring you back again.
To me, I own, it just seems daft
To leave a working, airborne craft,
But three o' clock, right on the dot,
Fiona, Dave, the priest, the lot
All jumped into the sky-blue void.
(I'll tell you something: Sigmund Freud
Would have a field day with this shower;
He'd keep them on the couch for hours –
Death wish/nuptials intermixed,
Bliss for a psychiatrist.)

High above the grazing cows
They screamed their solemn wedding vows,
And when all the 'I do's were done
They pulled their ripcords, one by one.
So gentle was the priest's descent,
He read the Bible as he went.
Alas for Fi and Dave, their luck
Was out. Their ripcords both got stuck,
And where you'd find their backup chutes
Most days, they'd stowed some champagne flutes.
And so it was that man and wife
Together exited this life.
What's writ hereunder clarifies
The moral of their sad demise:
For weddings, church is best by far
Or – at a pinch – a registrar.

# PHILLIP, WHO TALKED ONLY
## IN MANAGEMENT SPEAK

In hell the devil has a list of jobs which take your soul
And Management Consultant is the first one on the roll.
A man, let's call him 'Phillip', had spent year on dreary year
In climbing up the ladder of exactly this career.
His constant blue-sky thinking and his client-centred style
Meant 'Phillip' rose proactively quite smartly up the pile;
His knowledge-based incentivising earned him quite a name
In the real-time user-focused matrix-implementing game.

The ugly pseudo-language soon became his standard speech;
He'd use it in the pub or down the dogs or at the beach.
His friends grew slowly weary of his charmless invitations
To three-stage, food-led gatherings with grape-derived libations,
His girlfriend almost left him when he made the bold request
For some value-added hands-on top-down sex before they dressed,
His mother, on her birthday, was appalled to get a card
Professing end-to-end robust emotivized regards,
And no one twigged he'd got a raise on hearing 'Phillip' say:
'I've levelled-up the monetising function of my pay.'

An outward-bound-style stag weekend just south of Bristol sealed
Phil's fate.  For, clothed in paintball gear while creeping through a field
And pondering his strategy, he didn't hear the sound
Of the farmer's combine harvester behind him, turning round.
As soon as 'Phillip' noticed the approach of the machine,
He stumbled and he tumbled and he hollered and he screamed
But though he called for help, it didn't do him any good,
For no one within hearing even nearly understood:
'Could someone please now optimise a bottom-line solution
And synergise their efforts to effect my restitution?
Engage a methodology repurposing your day,
Enabling as "action-item" hauling me away!'

And so it was that 'Phillip' was condemned to end his tale
As a bleeding-edge holistic drilled-down rolled-out human bale.

# ELLA, WHO DIETED HERSELF
# TO A SHOCKING END

When she glances in the mirror,
Ella sees a heffalump,
Jowly face and saggy belly,
Trunk-shaped legs and shelf-like rump.
She, of course, is quite deluded,
What she takes for monstrous thighs
Are, like all her other features,
Of exactly average size.

She, though, is the happy reader
Of the type of magazine
Favoured by the chick-lit addict,
It Girls, soap fans – that whole scene;
Manna for the body-conscious –
Stuffed amongst the perfume ads:
Articles on looking younger,
Diets, health regimes and fads.

'Drop Two Stone In Fifteen Minutes!'
'Binge Eat To Your Perfect Size!'
'Burn That Flab While Watching Telly!'
'Weight Loss Without Exercise!'
Snake oil free for every reader,
Nonsense clothed in cruel hope,
Quacks and fops dispensing wisdom
Woven from the oldest rope.

Ella finds herself entirely
Caught up in their weasel words.
What she sees as golden nuggets
Are, alas, just polished turds;
Notwithstanding that, her diet
Changes to accommodate,
Week by week, the sundry dicta
Scribbled by these reprobates.

First we find her eating shellfish,
Nothing else must pass her lips!
Week Two and she's junked the molluscs,
Gorging now on plates of chips.
Next up, seven days of detox
(Seaweed tea and algae bread
Taken hourly, as directed,
Eased down using low-fat spread).

Several days of parsnip dinners
Follow on from weeks of beans
(Every different type – you name it:
Butter, broad, borlotti, green . . . )
After that we find her larder's
Stocked with bags of curly kale –
This she eats with wholemeal pasta,
Sweetbreads, giblets, tripe and snail.

Not that this goes any way to
Helping her achieve her aim;
Nothing in the mirror changes,
What she sees remains the same.
Still, the girl is not disheartened,
Ella's made of sterner stuff:
Efforts must now be redoubled!
Time to make the regime tough!

Quite in thrall to her obssession,
Focused only on her goal,
Heedless of advice or warnings,
Ella loses self-control.
Patience gone, against convention
She begins to improvise,
Mixing bits from different 'experts',
Though she knows that isn't wise.

Offal from 'The Roman Diet',
Lentil cake from 'Sink or Slim!',
Silage from 'The Country Method'
(boiled with ryegrass, on a whim),
Gruel from 'The Dickens Programme',
Cabbage from 'The Green Regime',
Fungus from 'The Woodland System',
Chilli from 'The Tex-Mex Scheme'.

Cordon bleurgh, this noxious cocktail,
Eaten both for snacks and meals,
Means her poor, beleaguered insides
Know just how a dustbin feels.
After days of said concoction,
Ella's guts are in revolt:
First she hears a kind of creaking
Then, within, she feels a jolt,

Next there is a searing pain, her
Large intestine starts to bloat,
Springs right back, jumps past her lungs and
Wraps itself around her throat.
During Ella's strangulation
No one's there to heed her cries.
(Given how she smells post-prandium
This should come as no surprise.)

Thus it is, alas, that Ella
Bids the world a rasped adieu,
Throttled by her own intestine,
Sick of just digesting goo.
Should you want a moral, here's one:
Dieting's all good and fine;
Fads, though, can precipitate a
Swift and terminal decline.

# JEREMY, A WINE SNOB

There once was a wine snob named Jeremy Quest,
A Parker in corduroy trousers,
Quite possibly Great Britain's worst dinner guest,
*Non grata* in several houses.

He'd sit and he'd mutter, 'Sauternes? Ninety-four?
Good Heavens, man, what were you thinking?'
Or, 'Riesling from Germany? Dear me, I'm sure
It's intended for cooking, not drinking.'

He simply refused to drink any red wine
His host might have failed to decant,
But rather than simply politely decline,
He'd spit it out on to a plant.

He'd take trips to Threshers to laugh at the stock,
Behaviour most people deplore,
'Just look at this rubbish – I'd rather drink hock!'
He'd trill as he made for the door.

At his own dinner parties he wouldn't let in
Any bottle which didn't pass muster.
He'd take it and stride round the back to the bin,
Then wipe his hands clean on a duster.

It's said he once unwrapped the off-licence paper
To find it contained Jacob's Creek,
And suffered a violent attack of the vapours
So took to his bed for a week.

Now, Jeremy went to an on-the-spot tasting
At Château Couille down in Bordeaux.
Two sips passed his lips and he sniffed: 'Why I'm wasting
My time here, I really don't know.'

He flounced down a walkway, his nose in the air,
And tripped on the winery cat
(The animal sat there on purpose, I swear),
Lurched sideways and fell in a vat.

As Jeremy surfaced the third and last time
He glugged out these words: 'Dear me, oh
What a terrible manner of death! What a crime!
I can't abide Bordeaux Nouveau.'

His guts filled with Merlot, his Malbec-stained eyes
Rolled up as the Cabernet Franc
Burst each of his lungs and his liver likewise
And he turned slowly head down and sank.

The vat was closed up and the must was fermented,
As was, of course, Jeremy Quest.
But odd as it sounds (and for 'odd', read 'demented'),
The wine performed well under test.

That year Château Couille was 'the best wine to grace
Shoppers' baskets', so Parker has said.
Who cares what he thinks — the point is it all tastes
Much better now Jeremy's dead.

# MYFANWY, WHO ANSWERED AN EMAIL
## FROM A NIGERIAN BANK MANAGER

Myfanwy got an offer in her email late last week
From Lagos Standard Bank Trust, which she felt was wholly sound.
To cut the story short, she's on the run in Mozambique
And she owes the British Treasury a hundred million pounds.

# BELINDA, WHO THOUGHT ANIMALS SMARTER THAN PEOPLE

Belinda's problem was her cat.
No, let's be fair – I should say that
The cat himself was good as gold,
The trouble was, if truth be told,
Belinda loved God's every beast
From North or West or South or East
Which crawled or flew or swam or ran,
The sole exception being Man.

People, on the whole, were base,
A compromised, degraded race –
Stupid, thoughtless, lacking wit
And not even aware of it –
But animals were gently wise
(At least through Bel's deluded eyes)
And none could quite as well prove that
As Athelstan, her treasured cat.

Belinda treated Athelstan
As though he were a little man:
She'd sit him on a chair to eat
With knife and fork strapped to his feet,
And, though a cat and only six,
She'd talk to him of politics,
Deducing from his puzzled looks
That he too thought the Tories crooks.

She'd take him places in her car,
Like bingo or the opera
(For which she'd dress him in a tux).
She read to him from Aldous Hux-
Ley, Dickens, Thomas Mann and such
As don't impress a feline much.
To those who scoffed she said, 'You'll find,
They're smarter far than humankind.'

All Athelstan desired was sleep;
To his chagrin Belinda'd keep
On waking him for his advice
On tax or clothes (though never mice,
For that's as much as to suggest
Such things are what a cat knows best).
Belinda would divine his views
From what she claimed were different mews.

Convinced that he was always right,
She asked him how to fit the light
She'd bought for hanging in the hall,
And guided by the tones of all
His angry yowls she chose the fuse
Which she believed he'd said to use.
She screwed it* in and thereupon,
Alas, she turned the hall light on.

According to the local news,
They only found Belinda's shoes
And, smoking gently on the floor,
A pile of soot – no less, no more.
Policemen took the cat away
And found him somewhere else to stay.
The neighbours clucked, her family wept
And Athelstan, at long last, slept.

In terms of morals, I can see
That here we have a choice of three:
The first, that cats are very smart
But resolutely black of heart.
The next, they're dumb and bound to make
The odd, albeit dire, mistake.
The last one's best: they're only pets,
That's why there are no feline vets.

# DAVEY, WHO COULD DO NOTHING WITH-OUT THE TELEVISION

Davey Trevithick relied on the telly
For every part of his indolent life:
They came round and tidied his house (it was smelly)
And when he was lonely, they found him a wife.

They sourced him a home in a far-flung location,
A quack came and told him just what he should eat,
Two harridans dripping with posh affectation
Unclothed him, and dressed him back up like a treat.

His children were shits, so he called a researcher
Who sent round a nanny as quick as a flash,
A woman in PVC reined in his lurcher,
A man from New York helped him manage his cash.

His mother was cross when he called her one Sunday
And rather than ask what the problem might be,
He drove his whole brood down to London that Monday
To thrash it all out live on morning TV.

In time, Davey found he was wholly unable
To function in any respect on his own,
His grip on his life grew a little unstable;
He couldn't survive long when left all alone.

His wife and his kids went away for a treat
And his whole life descended at last into farce –
He realised, whilst sat with his jeans at his feet,
That he wasn't quite sure how to wipe his own arse.

He phoned Channel 4 on his mobile. They told him
There wasn't a programme which covered his need,
But if it in any way helped or consoled him,
They liked his suggestion a great deal indeed.

Cut off from the wisdom of cheap television,
Without which there wasn't a thought he could have,
Davey Trevithick, to widespread derision,
Made headlines by starving to death on the lav.

# PAT, WHO TANNED HERSELF
## TO DEATH

Ah, I see your eye has rested
On my conversation piece.
Where's it from?  You haven't guessed it?
Here's a clue: it's from my niece.
How she came by such a chair
Bears the telling – sit right there.

Auntie Pat, my niece's mother,
Nice enough but rather dim,
Spent her life in showing others
Quite how brown she was, and slim.
Said she found eternal youth
In an upright tanning booth.

Sad to say, by age of fifty
All those ultra-violet rays
Made poor Pat look quite as if she'd
Best be served with *sauce béarnaise*.
Auntie Pat was urged to stop;
Outlawed from the tanning shop.

Heedless of her children's pleading,
Pat continued in this style,
Notwithstanding all the bleeding
Or the fact she looked so vile.
One day, as she bent her knees,
All her joints began to seize.

Skin all waxy now, like leather,
Age and ache began to show,
Bones quite worn and body weathered,
Auntie Pat began to slow.
Legs bent, back straight, head-in-air,
Pat looked every inch the chair.

That, you'll note, is how she perished
Ten years since, and now you sit
Upon a rare and deeply cherished
Heirloom. Novel, isn't it?
Now, do tell me what you think,
While I fix us both a drink.

# IVAN, WHO SHOPPED ONLINE

Ivan Grayling loathed December;
 'Look,' he'd say, 'you must remember
  All the panic, all the pain,
  All that trudging in the rain,
  All that schlepping round the stores
  Amid the crush of oiks and bores,
  Who bark your shins with bags and prams
  Whilst screaming at their little lambs
  To let poor Santa's beard be.
  In short, I hate it. Q.E.D.'

  So, being a resourceful man,
  One year he formed himself a plan:
  Eschewing shops and heaving streets
  And children high on Christmas treats,
  He chose instead to go online
  And – civilised, with glass of wine –
  Sat calmly in a comfy chair
  And ordered gifts from here and there,
 Thus never had to venture out
 To see what bargains were about.

An added bonus to this scheme
 Was: all the things that might have seemed
 Too heavy to be carried home
 When Christmas shopping all alone
 Were back in play; 'Some other clot
 Will have to hoik the bloody lot,
 Not me,' he chuckled, and at once
 Got searching and became ensconced
 In buying gifts of such a scale
 As sorely test the Royal Mail.

That year, the Grayling family's gain
 Would only cause the postie pain:
 For brother Tom, a set of weights,
 For Joan, two gross of china plates,
 Matilda got that man-sized gong
 She'd had her eye on for so long,
 For Charles, a fountain-building kit,
 For Little Jo, a roasting spit,
 For Keith, a marble bust of Shaw,
And all delivered to the door.

One morning Ivan's postman, Jack —
Stout of heart but weak of back —
Overburdened with a load
Was moved to break the Mailman's Code
And ring upon a punter's bell
To ask him nicely if he'd quell
This tide of megalithic gifts,
Which he alone had had to shift.
But Ivan, deeply unimpressed,
Merely laughed at Jack's request.

So still he'd order, still they'd come:
For Abigail, a kettle drum,
For Mike, a stuffed and mounted whale
(Discovered in an online sale),
For Jeremy, an ottoman,
For Kate, the Song of Solomon
Carved upon a limestone frieze;
This last had Jack upon his knees.
Now anyone could see *Chez* Grayling's
Postman was distinctly ailing.

The night that Ivan G. was found
Lying dead upon the ground,
The single witness said he saw
Only a shadow on the floor,
Shaped like a man, but strangely bent,
Groaning softly as it went.
Cause of death, the inquest said,
A heavy mailbag to the head.
Though no one has arrested Jack,
He can't have got far with that back.

I do not choose to moralise –
Surmise what you wish to surmise –
I'll simply add: this time of year,
Compelled to offer others cheer,
Some find such sentiments appal,
But Merry Christmas to you all.

# ACKNOWLEDGEMENTS

There really are so many names:
My editor, Nick Davies, James
A. Taylor (he who did the deal),
Rob Aslett (on whom every meal
Depends).  Of course my family –
A source of notes and love and tea –
The Addisons: Joan, Mike and Jo
And Jake (although he doesn't know
He helped, he did).  And every friend
Who took the time and pains to send
Advice, of whom especially
I ought to thank Ms Auriol B.
(And since you ask, the B's for Bishop).
Kudos, too, to Lauren Fisher
(Auntie Lol) for every text,
Suggesting whom I tackle next.
Last, not least, the flowing hand
Of Adam Howling, Gentleman,
Who finds supplies of style and grace
Stacked up in his pencil case.
Acknowledgements should all comply
With certain rules, which I apply
Quite happily to these, to wit:
The author ought to take the hit
For any part which you find rum
Or crass or dull or just plain dumb.
The parts you like, or maybe love,
I credit to those named above.